Andreas Kühnemann

NAS

**Building Your Own Home Server
NAS for Beginners
Quick and Cost-Effective
Part 1**

In this guide, we will focus solely on the essential steps for setting up TrueNAS® and configuring specific shares and users. We'll explain the basic installation, booting from a USB stick, and setting up a simple, functional NAS environment.

Detailed customizations and advanced features will not be covered here in order to keep the setup as simple as possible and avoid overwhelming the user.

The goal is to enable beginners to quickly set up a functional NAS server, equipped with basic SMB or NFS shares and user permissions.

Imprint

ISBN: 9798311262200
Proofreading by: Self-proofreading. AI
Illustration by: www.artbreeder.com
Cover graphic and content images: www.artbreeder.com
Imprint: Independently published
The author is responsible for the content. Any use of the material is prohibited without their consent. The publication and distribution are carried out on behalf of the author, who can be contacted at:Andreas Kühnemann, Strassacker, 87487 Wiggensbach, Germany

Disclaimer

The information contained in this document or on the pages and resources provided in this context is for general informational purposes only and serves as a guide for setting up a NAS server. It is intended as assistance for using TrueNAS and related technologies. Any use of this information is at your own risk.

Data Loss and Liability:

The author and/or publisher of this material assume no liability for any direct, indirect, incidental, special, or consequential damages that may arise from the use of the information provided herein, including but not limited to data loss, loss of business revenue, or other financial damages. This is especially true for data loss during the setup or use of a NAS server, including the use of TrueNAS®, RAID arrays, disk configurations, and troubleshooting. It is explicitly pointed out that there is no guarantee for the integrity of the data stored on a NAS server. The use of RAID technologies for data backup does not offer complete security and may, in certain cases (e.g., hardware failure, human error, software error, natural disasters, etc.), result in data loss.

Data Backup:

It is strongly recommended that all users regularly back up their important data before proceeding with the configuration of RAID arrays or other data storage solutions. The author assumes no responsibility for data loss or the inability to restore data after a RAID recovery or system failure.

Accuracy and Timeliness of Information:

Despite efforts to keep the information in this document accurate and up-to-date, no guarantees are made regarding the completeness, correctness, or timeliness of the provided data. Changes or updates to the technologies, products, or procedures described may occur at any time. The author assumes no responsibility for typographical errors or technical issues that may be present in this guide.

Use of Software and Hardware:

The use of software and hardware solutions such as TrueNAS®, RAID arrays, hard drives, and NAS systems is governed by the respective licensing agreements and warranty conditions of the manufacturer. The author cannot be held responsible for any errors, defects, or complications that may arise from the use of these products.

Legal Provisions:

This disclaimer is to be understood in accordance with the laws applicable in your country. In certain countries or regions, specific legal provisions may limit or exclude the liability of the author or publisher in relation to data loss or other damages. By using the information and procedures described in this document, you agree to this disclaimer and acknowledge that you assume full responsibility for any risks associated with the use of these technologies.

End of Disclaimer

Notice Regarding the Protection of Intellectual Property Rights

All trademarks, logos, product names, and company names mentioned in this context are the property of their respective owners. The use of brand names or protected terms is solely for identification purposes and does not imply any affiliation or endorsement by the respective rights holders.

- Microsoft©, Windows© are registered trademarks of Microsoft Corporation.
- Rufus is an open-source software licensed under the GNU General Public License (GPL) Version 3. This means that Rufus itself is subject to the copyright of its developer, Pete Batard, and contributors.
- TrueNAS® is a registered trademark of iXsystems, Inc. All rights reserved.
- iXsystems® is a registered trademark of iXsystems, Inc. All rights reserved.
- Seagate® IronWolf® is a registered trademark of Seagate Technology LLC. All rights reserved.
- WD Red® is a registered trademark of Western Digital Corporation. All rights reserved.
- Intel® is a registered trademark of Intel Corporation or its subsidiaries in the U.S. and other countries.
- AMD Ryzen® is a registered trademark of Advanced Micro Devices, Inc. All rights reserved.
- Xeon® is a registered trademark of Intel Corporation or its subsidiaries.
- USB® is a registered trademark of USB Implementers Forum, Inc.

All mentioned trademarks, logos, and product names are the property of their respective rights holders. Their use is solely for identification purposes and does not imply any affiliation or endorsement by the rights holders. If any intellectual property rights have been inadvertently infringed upon, we kindly request notification so that a prompt and amicable solution can be reached.

By reading this book, the reader accepts that they have understood and acknowledged the disclaimers and terms of use outlined here. Any legal claims arising from the use of this book are subject to the laws of the Federal Republic of Germany, excluding the UN Convention on Contracts for the International Sale of Goods. The place of jurisdiction, as far as legally permissible, is the author's place of residence.

Note: A glossary of technical terms used in the text can be found at the end of the guide.

Containment

Foreword

In today's digital world, the need for secure and flexible storage solutions is continuously growing. Storing data on a central server that can be accessed by various devices on a network is a perfect solution for many personal and professional applications. However, not everyone needs to rely on expensive commercial devices or cloud services. What many don't know is that with a bit of time and the right guidance, you can turn old hardware into a powerful NAS server (Network Attached Storage) that meets these very needs.

In this book, we want to show you how to easily set up your own NAS server with TrueNAS – and even with hardware you may already own. Don't worry, you don't have to be a tech expert! Step by step, we will guide you through the entire process, from selecting hardware to configuring and using your new server. You'll learn how to create storage pools, configure shares, and make the server accessible for Windows, macOS, and Linux.

With TrueNAS® as a helpful tool and clear instructions, you'll be able to create a powerful NAS server that offers great flexibility and security for your data – all at a low cost, possibly even with no additional expenses.

Enjoy discovering and implementing your own NAS solution!

What is a NAS Server and What is it Used For?

A NAS server (Network Attached Storage) is a networked storage device that allows files to be stored centrally and accessed from various devices. Unlike an external hard drive, a NAS is independent and can be available 24/7 on the network. This makes it an ideal solution for data backup, media management, file sharing, and remote access.

A NAS can be used both in private and business environments. At home, it often serves as a central media library to provide photos, videos, and music to smart TVs, PCs, or mobile devices. Automatic backups for computers and smartphones can also be easily set up. In businesses, a NAS is frequently used as a file server, allowing employees to access documents collaboratively.

Modern NAS systems offer additional features like cloud synchronization, virtualization, camera storage for surveillance systems, and Docker containers for specific applications. Depending on the configuration, a NAS can be equipped with RAID technology to ensure data security through mirroring or parity.

With easy access via Windows, macOS, Linux, smartphones, and tablets, a NAS is a powerful, flexible solution for anyone needing secure, centralized data storage.

Required Hardware for a TrueNAS® Server:

Minimum Requirements and Recommendations

For beginners, a system with a dual-core processor, 8 GB of RAM, and 1-2 hard drives is often sufficient. I have also tested it with 4 GB of RAM, a 1.4 GHz dual-core CPU, a 120 GB 2.5" internal SSD, and a 500 GB 2.5" external USB hard drive, and it works well enough for a private NAS (meaning 8 GB and RAID are not strictly necessary).

However, if you want to build a more powerful setup for a business or large data volumes, you should invest in a stronger processor, at least 16 GB of RAM, and several hard drives. A NAS with TrueNAS not only offers high flexibility and data security but also a future-proof solution for your storage needs.

The required hardware for a TrueNAS server depends on the type of use and specific requirements. TrueNAS CORE and TrueNAS SCALE can run on various hardware configurations, but there are some minimum requirements as well as recommended specifications for better performance and stability.

Following the details:

Minimum Requirements for TrueNAS®:

Processor (CPU):

Minimum:

64-bit compatible processor

1.4 GHz Dual-Core CPU

Recommended:

Quad-Core or better (e.g., Intel i5, i7 or AMD Ryzen)

Intel Xeon or AMD EPYC for higher demands.

Memory (RAM):

Minimum:

8 GB DDR4 RAM

Recommended:

16 GB or more (especially for ZFS pools or virtualization)

32 GB or more for more demanding setups.

Storage:

Minimum:

1 hard drive for the operating system (SSD recommend-ed)

1-2 hard drives for data (1 TB or more per drive)

USB stick or SSD (at least 8 GB) for the operating sys-tem.

Recommended:

2 or more hard drives in RAID-1 or RAID-Z (ZFS) for in-creased data security

SSD for the operating system, HDDs for data storage (1 TB or more depending on needs).

Network

Minimum:

100 Mbit/s Ethernet

Recommended:

2 x 1 Gbit/s or 10 Gbit/s Ethernet for larger data volumes or multiple users.

Other

USB stick or SSD for the operating system (at least 8 GB)

Motherboard with SATA ports or SAS controller for connect-ing hard drives.

Recommended Hardware for Higher Performance and Larger Setups:

PROCESSOR (CPU):

Recommended:

Intel Xeon or AMD Ryzen Threadripper multi-core processors (at least 8 cores) for virtualization, larger data vol-umes, and more complex applications.

Memory (RAM):

Recommended:

32 GB or more (especially for ZFS and large datasets or VMs).

For ZFS, at least 1 GB of RAM per 1 TB of storage space should be planned.

Hard Drives:

Recommended:

SSD for the operating system (at least 120 GB or more)

HDDs or NAS-optimized drives (e.g., Seagate IronWolf or WD Red) in RAID-Z2 or RAID-Z3 for additional data securi-ty and performance.

SAS controller or RAID cards for larger setups.

Network:

Recommended:

10 Gbit/s Ethernet for higher data rates and complex applications.

Power Supply:

Recommended:

High-quality power supply (80+ Gold certification)

UPS (uninterruptible power supply) to protect against power outages.

Additional Recommendations for Optimized NAS Environments:

Hardware RAID Controller:

For more powerful setups, consider using a hardware RAID controller with cache, which can further boost the performance of your ZFS system.

Ventilation and Cooling:

Good cooling and airflow are crucial to avoid overheating and wear of components.

Backup Strategy:

A good NAS system requires a solid backup solution. Use additional hard drives or cloud storage to back up your data.

Preparation

The TrueNAS CORE® ISO image is not bootable directly when written to a USB stick. Instead, you need to transfer it to a bootable installer USB stick. Here's what you need to prepare:

Download the Correct ISO Image

You can download TrueNAS CORE® from the official website:

https://www.truenas.com/download-truenas-core/

Download the ISO image (e.g., TrueNAS-CORE-13.0.iso).

This file is intended for installation, not for direct booting from USB. Therefore, you will need to:

Create a Bootable USB Stick

Since the TrueNAS ISO does not boot directly from a USB stick, you will need to use a tool to create a bootable USB installer. Use "Rufus" on Windows for this purpose.

- Insert your USB stick (at least 8 GB).

- Launch Rufus and select the following settings:

- Device: Your USB stick

To make the TrueNAS® ISO image bootable on a USB stick, you can use the tool **Rufus**. Here's a step-by-step guide:

Step 1: Prepare the USB Stick

- Plug the USB stick into an available USB port on your PC.
- In the Rufus window, select the correct USB stick from the "Device" dropdown list.

Step 2: Select the TrueNAS ISO Image

- Click the "SELECT" button next to "Boot selection."
- Choose the downloaded TrueNAS ISO image that you want to transfer to the USB stick.

Step 3: Partitioning and File System Settings

- For the partition scheme, choose "MBR" if you want to boot on an older PC, or "GPT" for newer systems that support UEFI.
- Set the target file system to "FAT32" (this is usually the default option).
- Leave the "Cluster size" at the default setting.

Step 4: Make it Bootable

- Enable the "Quick format" option and ensure that the "Create a bootable disk using" option is set to "ISO image (recommended)."
- Click "Start."

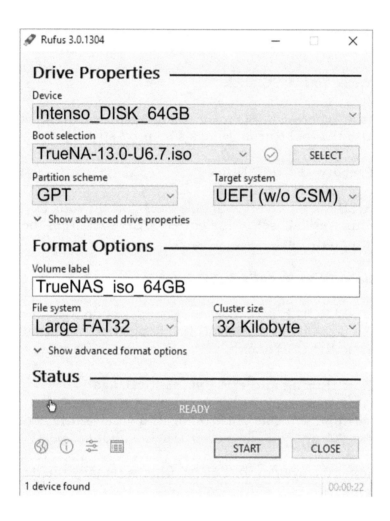

Step 5: Confirm and Wait

- Rufus will display a warning that all data on the USB stick will be erased. Confirm this and proceed.
- The process will now begin, and Rufus will make the TrueNAS ISO image bootable on the USB stick.

Step 6: Start the Installation

- Once the process is complete, insert the USB stick into the target computer.
- Restart the computer and go into the BIOS/UEFI to select the USB stick as the first boot device.
- TrueNAS should now boot from the USB stick, and you can continue with the installation.

That's it! You have now successfully made the TrueNAS ISO image bootable on a USB stick and can proceed with installing it on your NAS server.

Preparing the NAS Server

If you want to configure TrueNAS® without RAID, you only
need the following hard drives:

1. Boot Drive

You will need at least 1 hard drive (or an SSD) on which
TrueNAS® will be installed. This drive will serve as the boot
drive.
A drive with a capacity of at least 16 GB is usually sufficient
to install the operating system. If you need more space (e.g.,
for additional system files), you can choose a larger drive.

2. Data Storage Drive

You can use one or more hard drives for data storage. In a
simple setup without RAID, you will use the drives as individual storage drives.

Recommended: At least one additional hard drive for your
data, depending on your storage needs.

Minimal Hardware Requirements for Operation With-
out RAID:

- 1 hard drive (boot drive) for the operating system.
- 1 or more hard drives for data storage.

Example:

- 1 SSD or HDD for the operating system (at least 16 GB).
- 1 HDD or SSD for data storage where you will store your
  data.

Important:

If you use multiple hard drives but without RAID, the drives will not be mirrored or combined. Each hard drive will be used independently, and you will need to ensure you regularly back up your data, as there is no redundancy.

To build a TrueNAS® RAID server, you will need at least two DATA drives if you want to set up a RAID 1 (mirroring) array. Here's a detailed explanation:

Boot Drive

At least 1 hard drive for the operating system: You will need a hard drive or SSD to install TrueNAS® on. This drive will serve as the boot drive.
The size of the boot drive does not need to be large (usually, 16 GB or more is enough, but it depends on the TrueNAS® release and your requirements).

2. RAID 1 (Mirroring)

For the RAID 1 configuration (mirroring), where data is identically stored on two hard drives, you will need two hard drives.
These drives will work together to store the data redundantly. If one hard drive fails, the data will still be available on the other drive.

Minimal Hardware Requirements for RAID Operation:

- 1 hard drive (boot drive) for the operating system.
- 2 hard drives for the RAID 1 mirroring.

Example:

- 1 SSD or HDD for the operating system (at least 16 GB, more depending on needs).
- 2 identical hard drives (HDDs or SSDs) for the storage pool, connected as RAID 1.

So, if you want to set up TrueNAS® with a RAID 1 mirroring, you will need at least 3 hard drives: 1 for the boot drive and 2 for the data RAID.

If you want to use RAID 0 (no mirroring but higher speed), you will need at least 2 hard drives as well.

Expansion:

For more data security and performance, you can also configure RAID-Z or RAID-Z2 (ZFS), which requires additional hard drives.

To install a second or third hard drive in your NAS server, certain hardware knowledge is required, but it is a relatively simple process. If you haven't done so yet, you will need at least a second hard drive to function as the data drive. The first drive should be the boot drive, and it can be smaller since it only stores the operating system and basic system files.

Step 1:

Turn off the PC and disconnect the power. Then open the NAS server or PC case to access the hard drive slot.

Step 2:
Install the second hard drive by inserting it into the designated slot and connecting it with the SATA and power cables.

Step 3:
Start the PC and enter the BIOS to ensure the hard drive is detected. Afterward, you can set it up in the operating system and configure it as the data drive.

Now you have two hard drives: one for the operating system and one for the data.

Boot TrueNAS and Install:

Boot from the USB stick: Insert the USB stick into the NAS server, enter the BIOS (usually with F2, DEL, or F12 at startup), and set the USB stick as the boot source.
Install TrueNAS CORE: In the boot menu, choose the installation and follow the instructions to install TrueNAS on a separate hard drive or SSD (not on the USB stick itself).

Summary:

The TrueNAS ISO is not directly bootable; you need to write it to a USB stick.

Tools like Rufus (Windows) or dd (Linux/macOS) help you create a bootable installer.
After the installation, TrueNAS will boot from the hard drive/SSD, not from the USB stick.

The Setup

Here's an easy-to-follow guide on how to install TrueNAS®
on a server and complete the first boot process, including
the prompt with the NAS server's IP address.

Preparation: Before starting the first boot, make sure that
you've transferred the TrueNAS® ISO image to a bootable
USB stick (e.g., using Rufus). Your USB stick should be correctly set up and ready to boot from on the server.

Step 1:

Connect the USB Stick and Power On the Server

1. **Insert the USB Stick**: Plug the USB stick containing the
   TrueNAS® ISO image into an available USB port on the
   server.
2. **Power On the Server**: Turn on the server. Make sure the
   server boots from the USB stick. If the server doesn't boot
   from the USB stick automatically, go into the server's
   BIOS/UEFI (usually by pressing F2, F12, or DEL during the
   startup process).

• In the BIOS/UEFI menu, adjust the boot order so that the
  USB stick is set as the first boot device.
• Save the changes and restart the server.

Step 2:

Start the TrueNAS® Installation

TrueNAS® Installation Menu: Once the server boots from the USB stick, the TrueNAS® installation menu will appear.

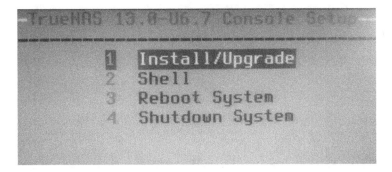

You will be greeted with a selection of options, including the installation mode and other configuration options.

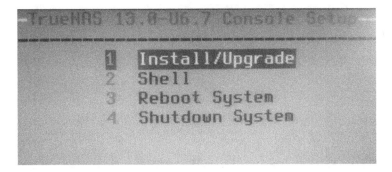

Select Install: Use the arrow keys to choose the "Install/Upgrade" option and press Enter to confirm.

Language Selection: A screen will appear for language selection. Choose your desired language (usually English) and confirm by pressing Enter.

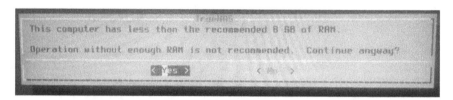

I tried it with 4GB of RAM, and it works flawlessly; this should be sufficient for basic server services.

Step 3: Select the Disk for Installation

Select Disk: The installation process will prompt you to choose the disk where you want to install TrueNAS®. This is typically done on the first disk (the boot drive).

Select the Disk: Choose the disk that will serve as the boot drive (this is typically a smaller SSD or HDD).

Warning: All data on this disk will be deleted. Make sure you select the correct disk!

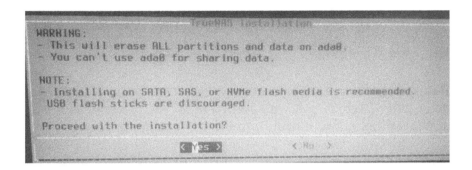

Installation Confirmation: After selecting the disk, TrueNAS® will ask for confirmation that you want to erase the disk and install TrueNAS® on it. Confirm by selecting "Yes."

BIOS Selection: Use BIOS here, not UEFI, as this is better supported. UEFI is only supported on newer motherboards.

Step 4:

Install TrueNAS®

1. **Installation Process**: The installation process will now begin. TrueNAS® will install the system on the selected disk. This may take a few minutes.
2. **Installation Complete**: After the installation is complete, you will be prompted to reboot the server. Remove the USB stick when prompted to ensure the server boots from the hard drive.

Step 5:

Reboot the Server and Initial Configuration

This will take a bit of time as the boot drive will now be checked. You will see several rows with (.) and (+) symbols. This process will take about 5-10 minutes.

Reboot the Server: The server will now boot from the hard drive where TrueNAS® was installed. A text-mode screen will appear, displaying information about your system.

Display IP Address: On this screen, the IP address of the server will be shown. This is crucial for later connecting to TrueNAS® via a web browser.

o   Look for a line similar to this:

Web Interface: http:// 192.168.115.111

o   Make a note of this IP address (the address may vary depending on your network, but it will always begin with http://192.168).

Step 6:

Access the TrueNAS® Web Interface

Open a Web Browser: On another computer in the same network, open a web browser (e.g., Chrome, Firefox, Edge) and enter the displayed IP address to access the TrueNAS® web interface. If you're using the IP address on this PC, it must start with 192.168.115.

Example: Enter the IP in the browser's address bar like this:

http://192.168.115.111

(Replace this with the actual IP of your TrueNAS® server).

If you haven't set a password yet, you will be prompted to create one. We used "**123456**"

Afterward, the login screen will appear.

Enter Login Credentials: After entering the IP address, you will be redirected to the TrueNAS® login page.

o   The default username is root
o   The default password is admin (It's recommended to change the password after the first login).

Step 7:

First Steps in the TrueNAS® Web Interface

Login: Log in with the username root and the default password admin.

Initial Configuration: After logging in, you will be directed to the TrueNAS® web interface for configuration.

Configure Disks and Set Up Pools

Check and Adjust Network Settings

Set Up Additional Options like User Management and Shares

Summary:

- **First Boot**: You boot TrueNAS® from a USB stick and install it on a hard drive.
- **Installation Process**: TrueNAS® is installed on the hard drive, and the server will then reboot.
- **IP Address**: The server's IP address will be displayed on the screen. You'll need this IP to connect to the TrueNAS® server via a web browser.
- **Accessing the Web Interface**: Enter the IP address in your web browser, log in with the default credentials, and begin configuring the server.

You are now ready to continue setting up your TrueNAS® server!

Changing Language Settings

After logging in, you'll be taken to the TrueNAS® dashboard. Click on your user profile in the top right corner (the icon with your username or avatar).

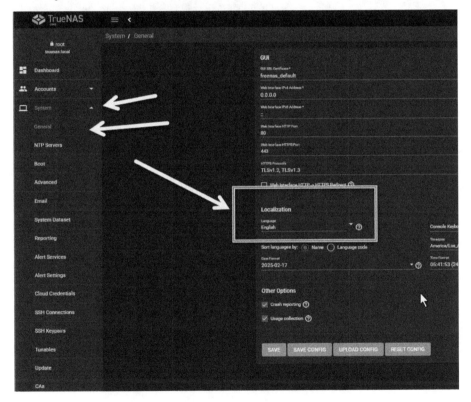

Select the "**Sytem**" menu item.

Under "**General**" you should find an option for the language. Select **German** from the list of available languages.

Save Changes

Click "**Save**" to apply the changes.

TrueNAS® should now be displayed in US/English.

This change only affects the web interface, not the system itself. When you restart TrueNAS®, you will see the interface in your language.

The TrueNAS® menu bar

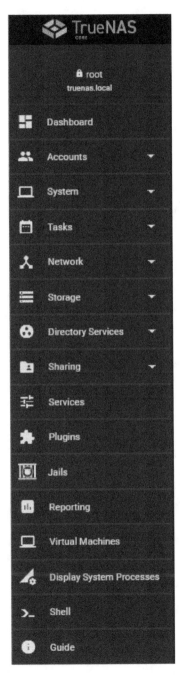

is the central control panel of the system. It is located on the left side of the user interface and provides quick access to all key functions. The menu bar is logically organized and divided into various sections to facilitate the management of storage, shares, users, networking, and system services.

The Dashboard provides an overview of the system status, while the Storage section allows the management of disks, pools, and snapshots. The Sharing section enables the configuration of network shares such as SMB (Windows), NFS (Linux), and iSCSI (virtual drives). Under Accounts, user and group permissions are managed, while Network handles IP addresses and connections.

Services such as SMB or FTP are activated in the Services menu. Additionally, TrueNAS offers automated backups, scheduled maintenance tasks, and extensions via plugins (TrueNAS CORE) or apps (TrueNAS SCALE). The menu bar provides an intuitive, step-by-step configuration process, even for less experienced users.

27

In Detail

Here is a detailed explanation of the individual menu items in TrueNAS®. These describe what you can configure under each menu:

Dashboard

o   What you can configure:
The Dashboard is the central overview of the status of your TrueNAS® server. Here, you can view various important system information, such as:
-   System status (storage space, CPU usage, network usage)
-   Disks (status and capacity)
-   ZFS pools and volumes
-   System logs and alerts
-   Current server activities
    You cannot make configurations here, but it helps you keep track of the overall status of your system.

2. **Accounts**
o   What you can configure:
Under "Accounts", you can manage users and groups that can access the TrueNAS® server. There are two main areas:
-   **Users**: Create, edit, and delete user accounts. You can set permissions and group memberships.
-   **Groups**: Create and manage groups, to which users can be assigned, in order to manage permissions for multiple users simultaneously.
-   **Passwords**: Change passwords for user accounts.
    These settings are essential for managing the security and access to your data.

3. **System**
o   What you can configure:
In the "System" area, you can make basic system and configuration settings for the TrueNAS® server:

- **General Settings**: Here, you can change the server's host-name and time zone.
- **System Log**: View system logs for troubleshooting and monitoring.
- **Access Control (ACLs)**: Defines who and how can access the system.
- **System Updates**: Install updates and patches for the operating system.
4. **Tasks**
   - What you can configure:
     This menu item is for managing scheduled tasks and cron jobs. Here, you can:
   - Set up scheduled tasks, such as backups or scripts that will run automatically at specified times.
   - Edit or delete existing tasks.
   - Define automations for various system processes, such as regular system checks or data backups.

5. Network

- What you can configure:
  Under "Network," you can manage the network connections and settings for your TrueNAS® server:
  - **Network Interfaces**: Configure Ethernet adapters (e.g., IP addresses, subnets, DHCP or static IP addresses).
  - **DNS and Gateway Settings**: Define the DNS servers and the default gateway for network access.
  - **Link Aggregation**: For network performance, you can combine multiple network interfaces into an aggregated connection.
  - **VPN**: Option to set up a VPN for secure access to the NAS from remote networks.

6. Storage

- What you can configure:
  In the "Storage" menu, you manage the physical and virtual storage devices on your TrueNAS® server:
  - **Pools**: Create, edit, and manage ZFS pools. This is where you decide how disks are combined in the system.
  - **Volumes**: Create and manage volumes that are used as data storage.
  - **Data Drives**: Assign disks and SSDs for specific functions or shares.
  - **Snapshots and Replications**: Configure snapshots to store a snapshot of your storage at a specific point in time, and replication for data backup and synchronization.

7. Directory Services

- What you can configure:
  Here, you can set up directory services like Active Directory or LDAP to centrally manage user administration and authentication:
  - **Active Directory**: Configure a connection to an AD server to integrate users and groups from an existing Windows network.
  - **LDAP**: Enables integration with an LDAP directory to control user access.
  - **Kerberos**: Configure Kerberos for more secure authentication.

8. Shares

- What you can configure:
  Under "Shares," you can configure access rights and protocols for file sharing:

  o **SMB (Samba)**: Set up Windows network shares.

  o **NFS**: Set up NFS shares for Linux-based systems.

  o **AFP**: Set up Apple shares (less common, but useful for older macOS versions).

  o **iSCSI**: Configure iSCSI LUNs to use the TrueNAS® server as an iSCSI target.

  o **Access Control**: Determine which users can access which shares and what permissions they have (Read, Write).

9. Services

* What you can configure:
  Under "Services," you can configure the various services running on your TrueNAS® server:

  o **SMB**: Enable or disable the Samba service for Windows shares.
  o **NFS**: Enable or disable the NFS service for Linux/Unix systems.
  o **FTP**: Enable an FTP server for transferring files.
  o **SSH**: Enable SSH for remote administration of the server.
  o **WebDAV**: Allows access to files via WebDAV.
  o Other network services like iSCSI, S3 (cloud storage), LDAP, or Rsync.

Summary:

These menu items offer comprehensive configuration options for the TrueNAS® server. You can manage users and shares, adjust network settings, set up disks and storage pools, integrate directory services like AD or LDAP, and activate various services like SMB, NFS, and iSCSI. Each menu item serves a specific aspect of managing and configuring your NAS server.

Creating Users and Sharing a Directory

The following steps are necessary to create a directory for "User1" and share it with a Windows user:

- **Log in to the TrueNAS® web interface.**
- **Create a new user.**
- **Create a new directory.**
- **Set permissions for the directory.**
- **Set up the share for a Windows user.**
- **Verify and test access.**

Chapter 1: Logging into the TrueNAS® Web Interface

If you have already done this, proceed to Chapter 2. If not: The first step in managing your TrueNAS® server is through the web interface, which allows you to control your server remotely. This section explains how to log in to the web interface to begin setting up your NAS system.

Find the IP Address of the TrueNAS® Server

To access the web interface, you need to know the IP address of your TrueNAS® server. This IP address can be found on the TrueNAS® server screen during the installation process. If the server is already running, you can determine the IP address either by using an attached monitor or through the command line:

1. Log into the TrueNAS® server directly, either using a monitor and keyboard attached to the server, or over SSH if you have enabled it.
2. To find the IP address, type the command ip a and look for a line showing an inet address (e.g., inet 192.168.115.111).

Open the TrueNAS® Web Interface in a Browser

1. Open a web browser (e.g., Google Chrome, Firefox, Safari) on your computer or laptop.

2. Type the IP address of the TrueNAS® server into the browser's address bar. For example, if the IP address is 192.168.115.111, enter:
http://192.168.115.111

3. Press Enter.

Troubleshooting:

• **Connection Failed**: If you cannot connect to the web interface, check the following:

- Is the TrueNAS® server powered on and running correctly?
- Did you enter the correct IP address? (Watch out for typos)
- Can you access the server from another device on the network (e.g., via Ping)?
- Is your web browser blocked by a firewall or security software?

Logging into the Web Interface

You should now see the login page of the TrueNAS® web interface.

1. On the login page, you will see two fields:
o **Username**: Enter root. This is the default administrator account.
o **Password**: Enter the password you set during the installation of TrueNAS® (**123456**). If you did not change the password, the default password is usually admin.
2. Click **Log In** or press **Enter** to log in.

Summary

Logging into the TrueNAS® web interface is the first step in configuring your server. You need to find the server's IP address and then access the user interface through your web browser. Once successfully logged in, you can begin managing your server, adding users, and setting up shares.

Chapter 2: Creating a New Pool in TrueNAS®

Creating a new pool on your TrueNAS® server is a fundamental step in organizing storage and making it available to specific users or groups. A pool helps you structure and manage your data. In this chapter, we will guide you step by step through creating a new pool.

Navigate to the "Storage" Section

After logging in, you will be taken to the TrueNAS® dashboard. On the left side, you'll see the menu bar with various options. Click on the "**Storage**" menu item. This will open the storage section, where you can make all the settings related to disks and directories.

Create a New Storage Pool (if not already created)

Before creating a directory, you need a storage pool. A storage pool is a collection of disks or drives grouped together to form a larger storage resource.

1. Click on "**Pools**" in the menu bar under the Storage section.
2. If you haven't created a storage pool yet, click on "Add" or "Hinzufügen". If you already have a pool, you can skip this step.

Follow the Wizard to Create the Storage Pool

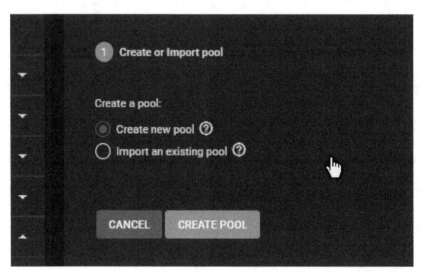

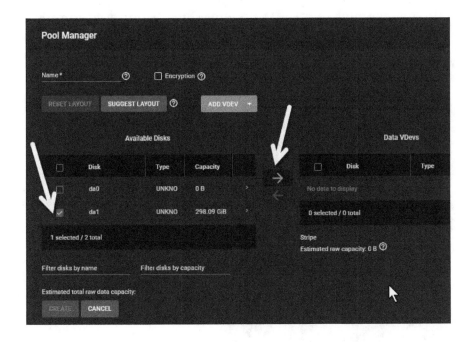

Follow the Wizard to Create the Storage Pool

Confirm the settings and create the pool by clicking the blue arrow. Now click on "**Force**" at the bottom left.

You will get a warning that a stripe is more susceptible to data loss, similar to a RAID system. Click "Continue" to proceed.

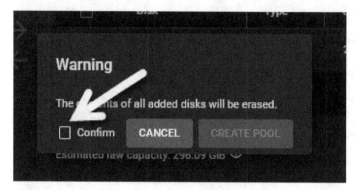

Click "Create" again, then confirm the warning window by selecting "Confirm." IMPORTANT: This step is often overlooked.

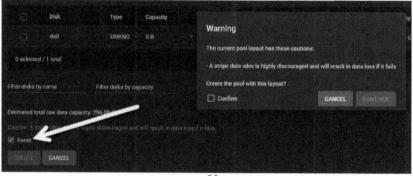

The pool is now created.

Create a new directory within the pool

After setting up your storage pool, you can now add a directory (also called a "Dataset"). The directory will be used to store files and folders.

- In the menu bar, go to **"Pools."**

- Select the pool in which you want to create the new directory.

- Click "Add" and then choose **"Add Dataset."**

- Click the "Add Dataset" button to create a folder (Dataset). This helps you organize the pool into different areas, such as "Accounting," "Media," "Backup," etc.

- Give the dataset a name, such as "Pool," and click "Submit/Save."

Configuring the Dataset

Now, a dialog will appear where you can configure the new dataset. You will need to make some basic settings:

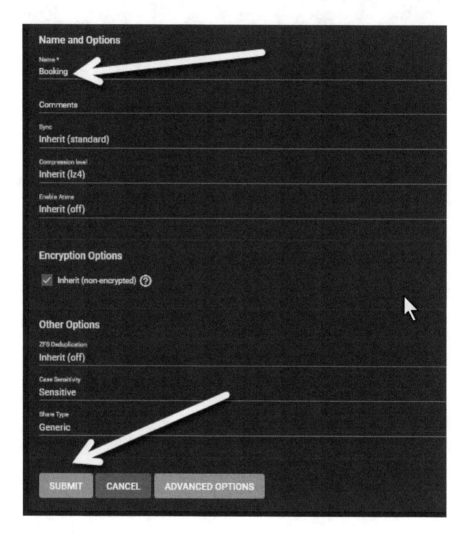

- **Dataset Name:** Give the new directory a name (e.g., **"Booking"** or "Accounting"). This will be the name of the directory you'll access later.
- **Compression:** You can choose whether to enable compression for this directory. Compression can save space, but it may sometimes reduce access speed. For beginners, we recommend leaving this option disabled for now.
- **Encryption:** You can decide whether to encrypt the directory. This is particularly important if you're storing sensitive data. If you don't have specific security requirements, you can leave this option disabled for now.
- **Access Control:** Later, you can set permissions so that only certain users or groups can access the directory. (This step is not covered in this beginner's guide.)

Once you've made all the necessary settings, click "Submit/Save" to create the dataset.

Set Permissions

After creating the directory, it's important to define the permissions so that you can control which users or groups can access this directory.

1. Go to "**Sharing**" in the menu bar and click on "**Windows Shares (SMB)**" if you want to share the directory with Windows users.
2. Click on "**Add**" and select the directory (dataset) you just created.

   This will allow you to configure the share settings and set access permissions for the directory.

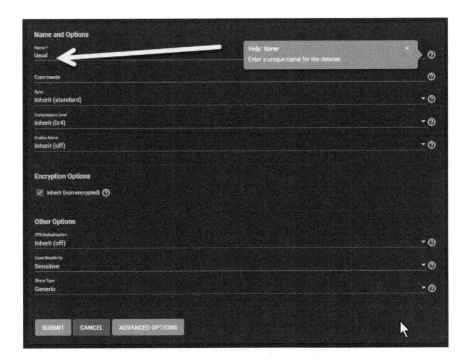

Select the directory that users will have access to. In the
menu bar > Sharing > Windows Shares (SMB)

1. After expanding the options, we selected "**TOSHIBA**" as the
   directory.

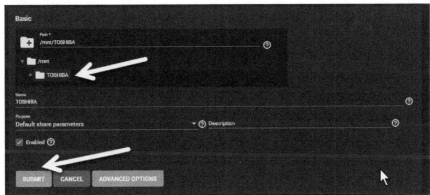

2. Under "**Purpose**", choose "**Multi-protocol (AFP/SMB) shares**".

For a Windows share in a private home network, **SMB (Server Message Block)** is the best choice. SMB was specifically designed for Windows and is easy to set up, secure, and compatible with macOS and Linux.

Why choose SMB for Windows?

- **Better Windows Compatibility**: Windows natively uses SMB for file and printer sharing.
- **Easy User and Rights Management**: Access can be controlled with user accounts and passwords.
- **Works with macOS & Linux**: If you plan to add macOS or Linux devices later, SMB works well with them too.
- **Fast & Secure**: It supports modern encryption and authentication methods.

Click "Submit"

Verify the settings

Once you've created the directory and set the permissions, you can verify if everything was set up correctly.

1. In the **TrueNAS® Web Interface**, go to the **"Storage"** menu and check if the new directory appears in your pool.

Troubleshooting:

- **Directory not visible**:
  If the directory is not visible, ensure that the pool was correctly created and that you created the directory properly. Check the sharing settings and permissions.
- **Access issues**:
  If a user cannot access the directory, verify the permissions and ensure that the user has the appropriate access rights (read/write) for the directory.

Summary

Creating a new directory in TrueNAS® is an essential step in organizing and efficiently storing your data. You can configure the directory according to your needs and share it with the appropriate permissions for users and groups. These steps will help you make the most of your storage space while controlling access, ensuring that only authorized users can access specific data.

Creating a New User in TrueNAS®

Creating a new user in TrueNAS® is an essential step for managing access to your server. You can set specific permissions for this user to ensure that only authorized individuals can access certain directories. In this chapter, we will walk you through the process of adding a new user.

Navigate to the "Accounts" Section

1. After logging in, you will land on the TrueNAS® dashboard. On the left side, you will see the menu bar.
2. Click on the "**Accounts**" menu item. This will open a dropdown menu.
3. From the dropdown menu, select "**Users**" This section allows you to manage all the users who have access to your TrueNAS® server.

Now, Add a New User

1. You will be taken to a page with a list of all existing users. To create a new user, click the "Add" button, usually located in the upper right (sometimes labeled as "+").
2. A form will appear, where you can enter the details for the new user.

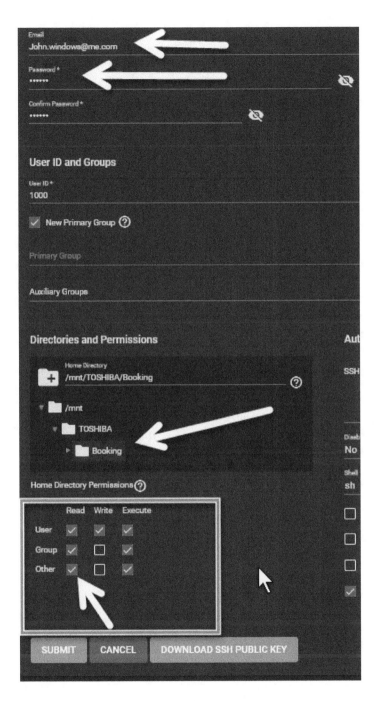

Email
John.windows@me.com

Password *
••••••

Confirm Password *
••••••

User ID and Groups

User ID *
1000

☑ New Primary Group ⑦

Primary Group

Auxiliary Groups

Directories and Permissions

Aut

Home Directory
/mnt/TOSHIBA/Booking ⑦

SSH

▼ ▣ /mnt
  ▼ ▣ TOSHIBA
    ▸ ▣ Booking

Disab
No

Shell
sh

Home Directory Permissions ⑦

	Read	Write	Execute
User	☑	☑	☑
Group	☑	☐	☑
Other	☑	☐	☑

☐
☐
☐
☑

SUBMIT   CANCEL   DOWNLOAD SSH PUBLIC KEY

47

Enter User Information

Fill out the fields in the form with the desired user information. Here are the key options you can configure:

- **Username**: Enter a unique username for the new user. This
  will be used to identify the user, we use **"jwindows"**
  o *(Usernames can be up to 16 characters long. When using NIS
  or other legacy software with limited username lengths, keep
  usernames to eight characters or less for compatibility.)*

- **Full Name**: Optionally, you can enter the user's full name
  for reference, we use **"John WINDOWS"**
- **Password**: Set a secure password for the user. Ensure that
  it's strong to maintain security, we use **"123456"**
- **Home Directory**: Define the home directory where the user's files will be stored. By default, this is usually set to
  /mnt/ but can be customized, in this case **"Booking"**
- **Shell**: Choose the user's default shell. For most users,
  /bin/csh is typical, but you can set it to a different shell if
  needed.

Setting Permissions for the User

For each user or group you add, you can set three basic permissions:

- **Read**: The user or group can view the files in the directory
  but cannot make any changes. This is useful if you want to
  share data for viewing only.

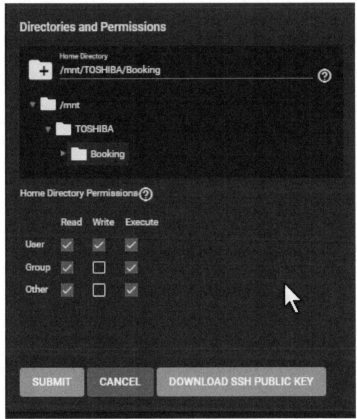

- **Write**: The user or group can read the files in the directory
  and also create new files, modify existing ones, or delete

files. This permission should only be granted to trusted users as it provides full access to the contents.
- **Modify**: This allows the user or group to make changes to the files but not perform basic directory operations (e.g., delete or move the directory). This is a more restrictive permission compared to "Write."

Permission Options

- **Owner**: This is the user who owns the directory and by default has the highest level of permissions. You can change the owner by selecting a different user here.
- **Group**: You can assign a group of users specific permissions for the directory.
- **Other**: These are all other users who are neither part of the group nor the owner. You can control access for users who don't belong to the specified group or the directory's owner.

Setting the Directory (Home Directory)

- **Home Directory**: This is where you can create a personal directory for the user. If you don't specify a directory, a default directory will be created for them.
- Choose a path for the user's home directory. If the directory already exists and matches the username, it will be set as the user's home directory. If the path doesn't match a subdirectory corresponding to the username, a new subdirectory will be created.

The full path to the user's home directory will be displayed when you edit the user.

Set Permissions

Make sure to enter the permissions for the new user. These are typically set correctly by default, but ensure the following options are selected:

- **Read**
- **Write**
- **Execute**

Activate all these permissions.

After you have set the permissions, click "**Save**" to create the new user.

Assigning User Permissions and Groups

Once you've created the user, you can assign specific permissions and groups to define what resources they can access.

1. Set Permissions

- Go to the "Shares" section (e.g., SMB or NFS) and assign **read** or **write** permissions for specific directories or folders to the user.
- 2. **Add to Group**

   You can add the user to existing groups like **admin** or **users**. Groups allow you to assign the same permissions to multiple users at once.

   Verify User Setup

   Once the user has been created and added to groups, you can verify the setup by accessing the shared directories from a Windows PC.

1. **Open Windows Explorer**
   o Press **Windows + E** to open the file explorer.

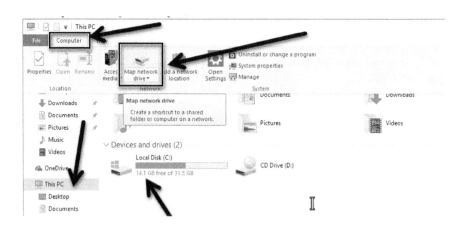

Map Network Drive

Enter the IP address of your TrueNAS® server, and you should see a list of shared directories that you've configured. You can then connect to the shared folder from your computer.

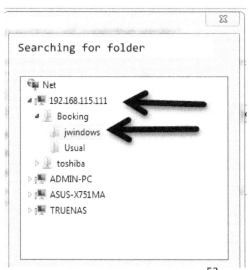

53

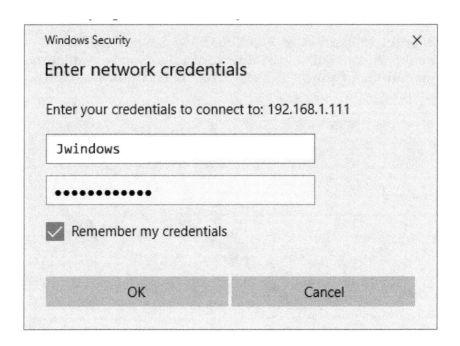

User Created:

- **Username:** jwindows
- **Password:** 123456

Make sure to update the password to a more secure one later for security reasons!

If you've done everything correctly

CONGRATULATIONS! 🎉

You should now have a working connection. In Windows Explorer, you can manage files just like on your PC, create folders, copy files, delete them, and more.

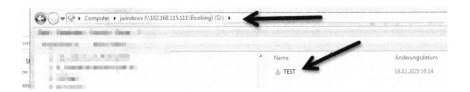

Summary

Setting permissions in **TrueNAS®** is a crucial step to ensure that only authorized users can access specific data. You can customize permissions for users and groups, specifying whether they can **read, write, or modify** data. Additionally, SMB allows you to configure permissions for **Windows users**, making it easy to share directories securely. With this **detailed control over access**, you can keep your data **safe

Reports

The **Reports** menu (**Dashboard > Menu Bar > Reporting**) is a crucial tool for **monitoring and diagnosing** your system. It helps you detect issues early and continuously check the **health and performance** of your TrueNAS server.

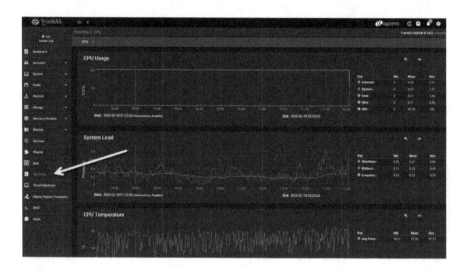

Here, you can view all **system logs** generated during TrueNAS operation. These logs provide insight into **system events, error messages, and other relevant activities** running in the background.

Error Descriptions

If you're having trouble **connecting to your TrueNAS server** via a network drive (e.g., SMB), various errors may occur. Below is an **alphabetical list** of possible issues, along with explanations and potential solutions:

Authentication Error

♦ **Cause**: Incorrect user credentials.
♦ **Solution**:

- Verify that the **username and password** are correct.
- Ensure that the **TrueNAS user has the proper permissions** for the shared folder.
- Double-check for **typos** in the username or password.

- **Blocked Firewall**

  ♦ **Cause**: The firewall is blocking access to the SMB share.
  ♦ **Solution**:

- Check the **firewall settings** on the TrueNAS server to ensure **SMB (Port 445)** is allowed.
- Verify the **client firewall settings** to ensure it isn't blocking SMB traffic.
- If needed, **add an exception for SMB** in the firewall settings.

Client Cannot Find the Shared Folder

◆ **Cause**: The client cannot detect the SMB share on the network.

◆ **Solution**:

- Ensure that the **TrueNAS server** is on the **same network** as the client.
- Check if the **SMB service** is running on the TrueNAS server.
- **Ping** the IP address of the TrueNAS server from the client to verify its availability.
- Try accessing the share **directly via the IP address** (e.g., \\192.168.115.111\booking).

- **DNS Issues**

  ◆ **Cause**: The client cannot reach the TrueNAS server using its hostname.

  ◆ **Solution**:

- Use the **IP address** instead of the hostname to bypass DNS issues.
- Ensure that the **TrueNAS server is correctly registered in the DNS server** and has the correct **IP address assigned**.

External Hard Drive Not Recognized

✦ **Cause**: An external hard drive meant to be shared is not recognized or not properly connected.
✦ **Solution**:

- Verify that the **external hard drive is properly connected** to the TrueNAS server.
- Ensure that the drive is **formatted and mounted correctly** in TrueNAS.

Check if the **file system is supported** by TrueNAS (e.g., **NTFS may not be natively supported**).

Incorrect Share Configuration

✦ **Cause**: The SMB share is not correctly set up, or permissions are misconfigured.
✦ **Solution**:

- Open the **TrueNAS web interface** and review the **share settings**.
- Ensure that the **user trying to access the share has the required permissions**.
- Check the **SMB share configuration** and confirm that it is **enabled and properly structured** with the correct permissions.

IP Conflict

◈ **Cause**: A conflicting IP address is preventing the connection.
◈ **Solution**:

- Check if another device on the network is using the **same IP address** as the TrueNAS server.
- If using **DHCP**, ensure that the TrueNAS server is assigned a **static IP** or is properly configured within the DHCP range.

- **Mount Errors** (Linux)

  ◈ **Cause**: Issues when mounting the SMB share on a Linux client.
  ◈ **Solution**:

  Ensure that the **cifs-utils** package is installed on the Linux client:

  Verify the **mount command** and ensure the **username and password** are correctly specified.

  Make sure the **mount path exists and is accessible**.

  ### Network Issues

  ◈ **Cause**: Problems with network connectivity prevent access to the TrueNAS server.
  ◈ **Solution**:

- Ensure the **TrueNAS server and client are in the same subnet**.
- Test connectivity using **ping** between the client and server:
- Check if the **router or switch** is functioning properly and **not causing connection issues**.

Port Blocking

- ◆ **Cause**: The required port (e.g., 445 for SMB) is blocked.
- ◆ **Solution**:

- Verify that **Port 445** (used for SMB) is open on both the **TrueNAS server and the client**.
- Ensure that **no firewall** is blocking SMB traffic.
- Check that the **router allows SMB traffic** through its firewa

- **Incompatible SMB Version**

    Cause: The SMB version being used is incompatible between the client and server.

    Solution:

- Ensure that the **SMB version** on TrueNAS is correctly con-figured. TrueNAS typically supports **SMB2** and **SMB3**, while **SMB1** should be disabled for security reasons.
- Check the **SMB version** on the client (Windows 10 and newer generally use SMB2 or SMB3).
- In TrueNAS, you can adjust the SMB version in the **share settings** to ensure compatibility.

TrueNAS Service Not Active

Cause: The SMB service on the TrueNAS server is not active or not configured properly.

Solution:

- Ensure the **SMB service** is active on the TrueNAS server. You can do this via the TrueNAS web interface.
○ Navigate to **Services** in the TrueNAS web interface and verify that **SMB** is running.
- If the service is stopped, restart it and check if it functions correctly.

Time Synchronization Issues

Cause: Time differences between the client and server can cause connection issues, such as authentication errors.

Solution:

- Make sure both the **TrueNAS server** and the **client** are synchronized with an **NTP (Network Time Protocol)** server.
- Verify the system time on both devices to ensure they match.

Connection Timeout

Cause: A long delay during the connection process can result in a timeout error, preventing the client from establishing a connection.

Solution:

- Investigate potential **network issues** such as:
  ○ Overloaded network connections.
  ○ High network latency or instability.
- Try restarting both the **server** and the **client** to eliminate any temporary connection problems.
- Ensure that no other network problems (e.g., routing issues or packet loss) are affecting the connection.

Access Permissions

Cause: The user does not have the correct permissions to access the share.

Solution:

- Check in the **TrueNAS web interface** to ensure the user has the correct permissions for the share.
- If groups were used, verify that the group the user belongs to also has the necessary permissions to access the share.

- **Backup via Command Line (Command Window)**

  Here is a simple example of creating a backup that can be
  triggered by an icon on your desktop. Knowledge of the
  Command Window is required.

  To create a simple backup of multiple directories on your
  TrueNAS® server, you can use a **batch file**. This file will be
  executed in the Command Window to copy files from your
  Windows PC to the NAS server. Older files will be automatically overwritten to ensure that only the latest versions are
  on the NAS.

  Preparations:

  Ensure that:

- Your **TrueNAS® server** is properly configured and accessible
  via **SMB protocol**.
- You know the **IP address** and **share path** of your NAS server
  (e.g., \\192.168.115.111\booking).
- You are aware of the **directories to back up** on your Windows PC (e.g., C:\files, C:\Documents).
- **Creating the Batch File:**

  Step 1: Open the Notepad Editor

- Press **Windows + R**, type **notepad**, and press **Enter**.

Step 2: Write the Batch Commands

- Enter the following commands to perform the backup and ensure old files are overwritten:

@echo off
xcopy "C:\Files" "\\192.168.115.111\booking" /E /H /Y
xcopy "C:\Documents" "\\192.168.115.111\booking" /E /H /Y
echo Backup completed!
pause

Explanation:

- xcopy: Copies files and directories, including subdirectories.
- "C:\Files" and "C:\Documents": The local directories to back up.
- "\\192.168.115.111\POOL\Buchhaltung": The network path of the TrueNAS share.
- /E: Copies all subdirectories, including empty ones.
- /H: Copies hidden files.
- /Y: Overwrites files without prompting.

Step 3: Save the Batch File

- After entering the commands, save the file with a .bat extension (e.g., **backup.bat**).
- You can save it to the desktop or any other convenient location for easy access.

Step 4: Run the Batch File

- Double-click the **backup.bat** file you created to run the backup process.

- It will automatically copy the files from your PC to the specified **TrueNAS share** and overwrite old versions.

- **Saving the File**

  Save the file with a .bat extension. In the editor, go to **File > Save As** and enter the filename, e.g., Backup.bat. Make sure toset the file type to **All Files** and add .bat at the end.

  ## Creating a Desktop Icon for the Batch File:

  Step 1: Create the Shortcut

- Navigate to the folder where you saved the batch file (e.g., C:\Users\YourUsername\Documents).
- Right-click on the batch file Backup.bat and select **Send to > Desktop (create shortcut)**.
- A new icon named Backup.bat - Shortcut will appear on your desktop.

  Step 2: (Optional) Change the Icon

  If you want to change the icon for the shortcut:

- Right-click the new desktop icon and select **Properties**.
- Click on **Change Icon...**.
- Choose a new icon or upload your own.

  Step 3: Test the Shortcut

- Double-click the desktop icon to run the backup.

- If everything is set up correctly, the backup process will begin, and you'll see a confirmation message at the end of the process.

- **Automating (Optional)**

  You can also automate the batch file to run at regular intervals using **Task Scheduler**:

- Open **Task Scheduler** from the Start menu (search for "Task Scheduler").
1. Click **Create Task**.
2. Give the task a name (e.g., "Backup to NAS").
3. Select the triggers to start the task regularly (e.g., daily or weekly).
4. Under **Action**, select the batch file Backup.bat.
5. Save and close the Task Scheduler.

  Now, the backup will run automatically at the scheduled time.

Summary:

- You created a batch file to back up multiple directories from your Windows PC to the NAS server.
- Using **xcopy**, you ensure that old files are overwritten.
- You created a shortcut on your desktop to run the backup with a single click.
- (Optional) You can automate the backup process using **Task Scheduler** so that it runs at a specific time.

Alphabetical List of Technical Terms and Abbreviations

- **Active Directory (AD)**: A Microsoft directory service used to manage user accounts and devices in a network. TrueNAS can integrate with Active Directory for user authentication.
- **ACL (Access Control List)**: A list of permissions that control who can access specific resources (files, folders) and what rights they have.
- **Btrfs**: A file system that can be used in TrueNAS for data storage. It offers advanced features like snapshots and subvolumes.
- **Boot Pool**: The storage area that contains the operating system and configuration files of TrueNAS. Typically configured on a separate drive.
- **CLI (Command-Line Interface)**: An interface where users enter commands in text form to interact with TrueNAS. It is an alternative to the graphical user interface (GUI).
- **CIFS (Common Internet File System)**: A network protocol used for file access in Windows-based networks. TrueNAS supports CIFS for file sharing.
- **Cloud Sync**: A feature that allows data to be synchronized between TrueNAS and cloud storage solutions (e.g., Amazon S3, Google Drive).
- **Dataset**: A collection of data created within a ZFS pool. Datasets in TrueNAS can be treated as separate volumes with different attributes such as storage usage and permissions.
- **Data Protection**: TrueNAS offers features like ZFS snapshots and replication to protect data from loss.
- **Deduplication**: A process that identifies and removes redundant data on the disk to save storage space. ZFS supports deduplication, but it is often used cautiously due to high resource demands.
- **iSCSI (Internet Small Computer System Interface)**: A network protocol that allows SCSI-based storage devices to be accessed over IP networks. TrueNAS can provide iSCSI LUNs to present storage as a block device to another server.
- **Encryption**: The ability to encrypt data on the disk to protect it from unauthorized access. TrueNAS supports encryption at the dataset level.
- **File Sharing**: The ability to provide files over the network. TrueNAS supports various file-sharing protocols like SMB, NFS, AFP, and WebDAV.
- **FreeNAS**: The predecessor of TrueNAS, also an open-source NAS operating system. TrueNAS is the newer, more developed version, offering additional features and an improved user interface.

- **Fault Tolerance**: The ability of a system to remain functional even in the event of hardware failures. ZFS, used by TrueNAS, provides built-in error correction and redundancy.
- **GUI (Graphical User Interface)**: The graphical interface of TrueNAS, where users can configure and manage the system. The same functions can also be executed via the command line (CLI).
- **Growable Dataset**: A dataset that can dynamically expand to use available storage space without requiring manual adjustments.
- **Hypervisor**: Software that manages virtual machines on a physical server. TrueNAS supports virtualization with Bhyve, the integrated hypervisor of FreeBSD (on which TrueNAS is based).
- **HDD (Hard Disk Drive)**: Hard disk drives used as storage media in a TrueNAS system. HDDs offer larger capacity but are slower than SSDs.
- **iSCSI Target**: An iSCSI device provided by TrueNAS to make storage available as a block device over a network.
- **Integrity Checking**: TrueNAS and ZFS offer mechanisms to verify the integrity of data to ensure it is not corrupted or damaged.
- **Interface**: Refers to the network interfaces of a TrueNAS system. These can be used for various purposes such as host management or file transfer.
- **Jails**: Containers in FreeBSD (and hence in TrueNAS) that act as isolated environments for applications or services. These provide a form of virtualization without full virtualization overhead.
- **LUN (Logical Unit Number)**: A logical representation of storage presented over the iSCSI protocol. A LUN can be used as an iSCSI target in TrueNAS.
- **LACP (Link Aggregation Control Protocol)**: A protocol used to bundle network connections. It helps increase bandwidth and ensure redundancy of network connections.
- **Media**: Refers to storage media like hard drives and SSDs used in a TrueNAS array. TrueNAS supports different types of media for efficient data storage.
- **Mirroring**: A RAID technology where the same data is stored on two hard drives to increase fault tolerance. ZFS uses this technique to redundantly store data.
- **NFS (Network File System)**: A file system protocol that allows users to share files over a network. TrueNAS can use NFS to provide file shares on Linux and Unix-like systems.
- **NAS (Network Attached Storage)**: A storage solution that is accessible over a network. TrueNAS is a NAS solution suitable for both private and business environments.

- **Node**: A single server or node in a network involved in a cluster or distributed system. In TrueNAS, nodes can be used to scale storage resources.
- **Pool**: A storage pool is a container that groups multiple hard drives (or virtual volumes) in TrueNAS. Data is distributed across the drives to ensure redundancy and fault tolerance.
- **Protocol**: A communication standard for data exchange between computers. Examples include SMB, NFS, AFP, iSCSI, and FTP.
- **Protection**: TrueNAS offers various mechanisms to protect data, including snapshots, replication, and ZFS checksums.
- **RAID (Redundant Array of Independent Disks)**: A technique where multiple hard drives are combined to improve data security, speed, or both. ZFS in TrueNAS supports various RAID levels, such as RAID-Z (a ZFS-specific variant).
- **Replication**: The process of copying data from one TrueNAS system to another to ensure that copies of the data are available at different locations.
- **Root Dataset**: The main dataset of a pool, containing the root data of the entire system.
- **SMB (Server Message Block)**: A network protocol used for file sharing and print services, particularly in Windows-based networks.
- **Snapshot**: A snapshot is a point-in-time copy of the file system. Snapshots allow the system to be rolled back to a previous state and provide a quick way for data backup.
- **Storage Pool**: A pool in which physical and virtual disks are grouped together to function as a logical unit.
- **TrueNAS Core**: The open-source version of TrueNAS, based on FreeBSD, offering a wide range of storage and network services.
- **TrueNAS Scale**: A Linux-based version of TrueNAS optimized for scalability and virtualization. TrueNAS Scale supports containers (Docker) and Kubernetes.
- **Target**: A target device that provides storage over iSCSI or other protocols. In TrueNAS, an iSCSI target is a specific storage area made available over the network.
- **ZFS**: A file system and volume manager used in TrueNAS. ZFS offers features like snapshots, data integrity, compression, and easy management of storage pools.

iXsystems® – The company behind TrueNAS®

RAID Levels 1 to 60

RAID Level	Description	Advantages	Disadvantages	Usage
RAID-1	Mirroring – Data is identically copied to two disks.	High data security (mirroring). Simple to implement.	Higher storage requirements (50% of capacity is used for mirroring).	Often used in small NAS systems and for data backup.
RAID-2	Byte-level stripping with Hamming code for error correction.	Very high error correction capability.	High disk requirements. Very inefficient in practice.	Rarely used today.
RAID-3	Byte-level stripping with a dedicated parity disk.	Good performance for sequential read/write operations.	Bottleneck due to dedicated parity disk. Lower performance for random accesses.	Obsolete, rarely used today.
RAID-4	Block-level stripping with a dedicated parity disk.	Good performance for sequential read operations.	Parity disk as bottleneck. Slower write operations.	Rarely used, largely replaced by RAID-5.
RAID-5	Block-level stripping with distributed	Good balance be-	Slow write operations. Com-	Very common in

	parity blocks across all disks.	tween performance, data security, and storage space. Excellent for read operations.	plexity in recovery in case of failure.	NAS systems and servers.
RAID-6	Block-level stripping with two parity blocks distributed across all disks.	Higher data security than RAID-5 (tolerates the failure of up to two disks).	Slow write operations. Higher disk requirements.	Common in enterprise systems and large NAS systems.
RAID-7	Proprietary RAID model with caching and data compression.	Very high performance due to caching and data compression.	Expensive, proprietary, non-standardized. Complex implementation.	Obsolete and not widely used.
RAID-10	RAID-1 + RAID-0 (Mirroring + Striping) – A combination of RAID-1 and RAID-0.	High performance and high data security. Fast read and write operations.	Very high disk requirements (50% of capacity).	Common in high-performance servers and NAS systems.

RAID-50	RAID-5 + RAID-0 − Combination of RAID-5 and RAID-0 (striped RAID-5).	Higher performance than RAID-5, especially for write operations.	Requires more disks and more complex implementation.	Used in performance-intensive NAS systems.
RAID-60	RAID-6 + RAID-0 − Combination of RAID-6 and RAID-0 (striped RAID-6).	Higher data security than RAID-5 and RAID-10. Good performance.	High disk requirements as 2 disks are used for parity per array.	For enterprise systems and large NAS applications.